RESPECT
Through the Eyes of Children

RANDALL L. KINNARD

KINNARD, CLAYTON & BEVERIDGE
ATTORNEYS-AT-LAW
Nashville, Tennessee

Respect: Through the Eyes of Children

Copyright © 2014 by Randall L. Kinnard.
All rights reserved.

ISBN: 978-0-692-24915-4
Library of Congress Control Number: 2014913543

Published by:
Kinnard, Clayton & Beveridge
Attorneys-at-Law
The Woodlawn
127 Woodmont Blvd.
Nashville, Tennessee 37205

Book design by Janice Phelps Williams

All profits from the sale of this book
will be donated to the following charities:
Legal Aid Society,
Court Appointed Special Advocates for Children,
and
Prevent Child Abuse Tennessee.

Additional copies of
RESPECT: Through the Eyes of Children
are available at local and online
booksellers everywhere.

Trade sales and bulk discounts
are available from Ingram.

Front Cover Entry

Respect is when somebody is nice or taking care of someone or something. Think of respect as some gasoline for the car of life. So, show as much respect as you can in life.

Anthony Culp
Nolensville Elementary School

Foreword

Respect is more than just a word. It is a concept, and its meaning is universally understood. You either respect something or someone, or you don't. Even fifth graders understand this, as evidenced by what you will see in this book.

I have worked as a trial lawyer for 37 years, representing injured people. Over the course of my career I have noticed a disturbing trend: More and more lawyers have started to respect others less and less. My concern inspired a speech titled "R-E-S-P-E-C-T" that I've been giving to legal associations around the country for five years now. It emphasizes the urgent need for lawyers to act more civilly towards one another, in and out of the courtroom. Their response has been gratifying.

Randall L. Kinnard with prize winners, Susannah Loss (Grand Prize), Alexa Mitchell, Elijah Broadus, and Sam Ferrell.

However, the downturn in respectful attitudes extends far beyond one profession. Civility is in a state of societal decline across the board. In fact, it is the very root of our most critical issues. Lack of respect is the thread that runs through the current rise in bullying, domestic and child abuse, the horror of school shootings and many more of today's tragic headlines. It is a world-wide problem.

Wanting to do more to spread awareness about the importance of respect, I thought, "What better place to start than with our children?"

The book you hold in your hands is the result of the "R-E-S-P-E-C-T" Contest started by my law firm. We ask fifth graders to write and draw what respect is and what it means to them. Each year the top entries are recognized at a courthouse celebration with teachers, principals, students and friends. We give monetary prizes to the winners' schools and donations to charities chosen by the winning students.

As you will see, fifth graders have a lot to tell us about respect. Their responses are touching and thoughtful. It's my hope that as you flip through the pages, you will be both encouraged that respect is alive in our youngest generation and inspired to raise the bar on respect in your community.

Randall L. Kinnard

Respect means that when the teacher is talking or teaching, you should not talk. Also, don't talk about someone who doesn't have expensive clothes or clean, nice shoes because it doesn't matter what they have, it's about their personality.

Elijah Broadus

Respect-O-Meter

Respect is showing others that they
are above you in your heart...
When you respect someone, they will know.

Chloe A. Fisher
Clarksville Christian School

Most Important Word Ever

Respect to me means treating somebody very nice.
To me it seems like the Golden Rule in one word.

Jermese Hathorn
Minglewood Elementary School

POLITENESS

When people say "respect," I think of showing people hat you recognize them as a person worth your kindness. I also think it means to show politeness to others. You give your respect to your elders, your teachers, your friends, your family, and any other person on earth.

McGavock Cooper
St. Paul Christian Academy

No Respect

Respect

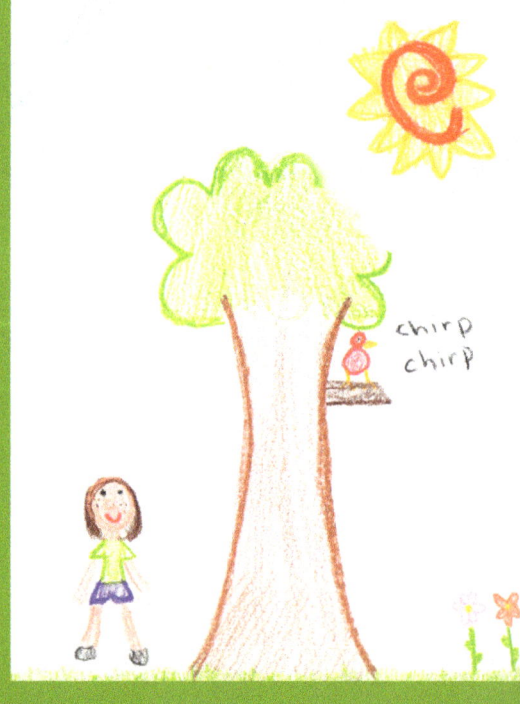

Susannah Loss
Meigs Middle Magnet School

REPAIR THE CRACKS

Without respect we can break people apart,
but together we can repair the cracks.

Emma Rutherford
Edmondson Elementary School

(AND PLEASE IS THE MAGIC WORD!)

show **R**espect... say hello
Empathy... say i'm sorry
Smile!... be happy
say **P**lease... it's being nice!
do **E**xtra work... it's being helpful
be **C**aring... it's being kind
Don't be **T**errible... show respect!

Respect means to treat with importance.

Arushi Mehta
University School of Nashville

Respect means to me how to show
a person that you have manners,
using words like thank you,
please, and excuse me.

Mariana Garcia
St. Edward School

NO RESPECT

RESPECT

Well, respect means ... everything to me.

Respect is important because if we don't have respect we don't have anything.

Alexa Mitchell
Apollo Middle School

Respect Builds Up

I think respect means stuff like your mom telling you to take out the trash and you do it the first time. That shows that you love your mother, and you're being respectful to her. Respect builds others up and makes you a good person!

Sam Ferrell
East Literature Magnet School

IT'S PARTY TIME!

What I think respect is, is treating people nicely. Like it's their birthday every day!

Braydn McCullough
Donelson Middle School

BE NICE TO OTHERS

Respect means to treat each other like you want to be treated and to be nice to others even if they don't look the same as you. Respect is important because if we didn't have it in our society, it would be destroyed and no one could forgive each other.

Kierston Bowles
Montgomery Central Elementary School

Respect turns us

Respect is how the world turns.
If there was no respect the world would be in ruins.

Emily Wood

Love Is the Heart of Respect

Love, which is the heart of respect, is important because if we want to be treated well we need to treat others the same. Also we need to have respect for the armed forces and the president.

Joseph Bellardo
St. Paul Christian Academy

CARE & KINDNESS

Respect is the care and kindness from a close friend or family member. It is important because people, who don't seem to have any of it from others, could really use it.

Caroline Patient
St. Edward School

Saluting Our Flag

Without respect there would not be any authority in our world. For example, saluting our American flag shows that we have respect for it, and without that it would not be as special to us as it is.

Ashlyn Clarke
St. Edward School

RELATIONSHIPS

I think respect is important
because it helps you to have a special
relationship with friends and family.
"Do unto others as you would have them
do to you," as I always say.

Clayton Tiller
Nashville Christian School

FOLLOW, DO, and LISTEN

Be home by ten 3.00 o'clock

Thank you for being on time 10.00

Respect means always follow directions or do the right thing and listen to your parent or teacher or guardian. Respect is the thing you need to get somewhere in life, because if you don't have it, it'll be hard finding a job.

Simon Robertson
J. T. Moore Middle School

EQUALITY

To me, respect means being treated kindly, fairly, and equally. I feel content, unique, and happy in a soothing warm form, when I am treated with sweet respect.

Eva Christopher
J. T. Moore Middle School

OPEN-MINDED

My idea is to eat ice cream every day.

My idea is to eat fruit every day.

Your idea is very nice. I like it better.

Thanks.

I think respect is being open-minded. I say that because when you are open-minded you listen to others' ideas and not so much stick to yours.

Naomi Taylor
Meigs Middle Magnet School

COME TOGETHER

LET'S HAVE R.E.S.P.E.C.T

- **R**IGHT
- **E**DUCATION
- **S**O
- **P**LEASE
- **E**VERYONE
- **C**OME
- **T**OGETHER

NO BULLYING

Respect means that you care about people and you have education. Respect is important because it makes people come together.

Wendy Martinez
Margaret Allen Middle School

BREATHE

BREATHE IN RESPECT

Respect is like oxygen. You need it in your life or you won't turn out well.

BREATHE OUT HAPPINESS

And when you breathe out respect, everyone is happy, because of all the respect.

*Emma A.**
H. G. Hill Middle School
* surname not provided

ALL PEOPLE, EVEN KIDS

HAVING RESPECT

I think respect is important because all people should have respect for everyone.

NOT HAVING RESPECT

Even kids should get and have respect.
It doesn't matter what race, color, or age.
We should still have respect for everyone.

Alexis Crite
East Nashville Magnet School

LISTEN

When people want respect, they are looking for many things, like attention, gratitude, and maybe even love.

In my opinion, what people really look for in respect is simply for other people to listen.

Katelyn White
Christ Presbyterian Academy

RULES = RESPECT

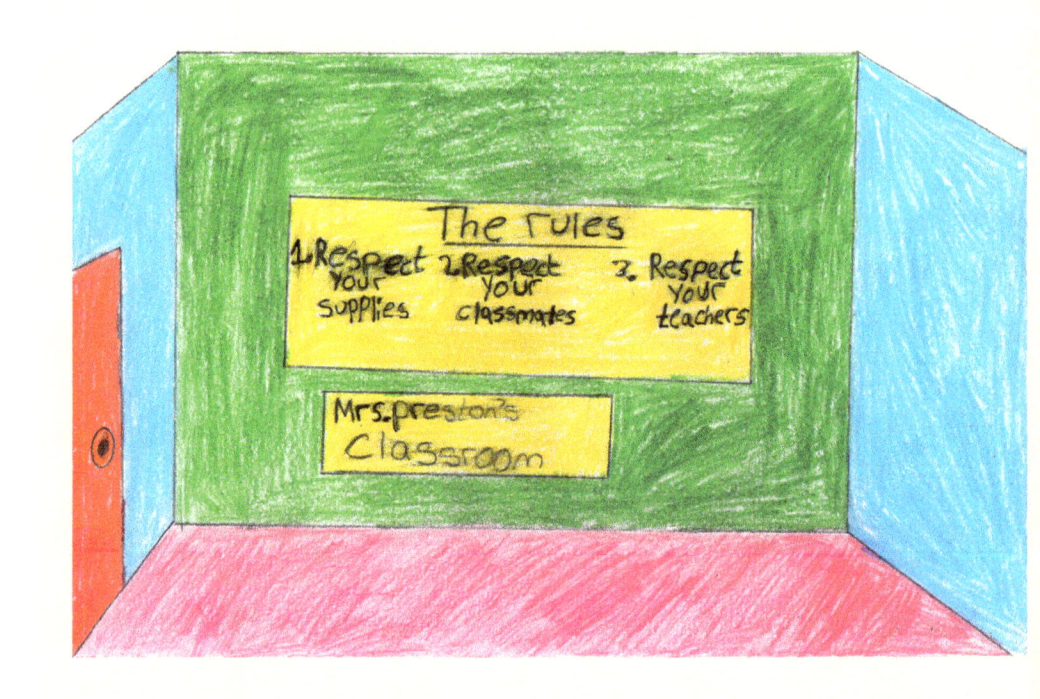

Respect is important because without respect there are no rules. Without rules, we are nothing. So, the word "rules" is just another word for respect.

Oscar Ekanem
Apollo Middle School

THE KEY

Respect is the key

To the lock of life

Respect to me is honoring your friends
and the people who provide for you.
Treat people how you want to be treated.

James Morrison
Battle Ground Academy

LIKE THE WIND

Respect to me is like the wind: cool, important, and not thought about a lot. But it is something that you should give someone every day.

Casey Crowe
Lipscomb Elementary School

AN OPPORTUNITY

Respect means to show someone you
care about them. It is a big opportunity
to show someone that they are
just as important as you are.

Haruka Shintani
University School of Nashville

BLESS YOU!

Respect is treating others the way you want to be treated! For example: saying "Bless you" when somebody sneezes.

J. D. Blier
East Nashville Magnet School

IT CAN CHANGE THE WORLD!

Respect means to treat your peers, friends, neighbors, and everyone in existence the way you would treat yourself. Respect means to make other people's days better, and I know it can change the world!

Tyler Bullock
Meigs Magnet Middle School

TAKING CARE

Respect is taking care of God's creation.

Emma[*]
Oak Hill School
[*] surname not provided

COURAGE

Respect is not a skill but something inside
your heart that can't be faked; something
that takes more courage to do than going to war.
That is what I think of respect.

Samuel Robertson
New Hope Academy

R-E-S-P-E-C-T

Respect is when you treat someone how you want to be treated. Respect is character! When I see respect, I think of the song "R-E-S-P-E-C-T." That's what it means to me!

Abigail Joseph
Apollo Middle School

DEEP IN MY HEART

It's from deep in my heart and sounds so easy, but respect is harder than writing a book and makes you have different emotions. This difficult thing is called respect.

Lily Ford
St. Paul Christian Academy

HONOR and HELP

Respect means to honor or give someone good self-esteem. It means to pick someone up when they're down, or even help someone when they have fallen. Sometimes when you're down and mad about getting second or third place, you need to congratulate the person ahead of you, because they're probably feeling happy. So, always give respect.

Ashley Graciat
Edmondson Elementary School

A LIFESAVER

Respect isn't just important, it can be a lifesaver.
No, not the candy, but respect is just as sweet.

Gracie Green
Lipscomb Elementary School

BEING THOUGHTFUL

Respect is being thoughtful to others no matter what they look like or what their religion is.

Gabriel Lewis
Barksdale Elementary School

IT IS IMPORTANT

I think respect is important because lately no kids show respect. Respect should be used in homes and anywhere else people should use respect.

Ilana Owens
Apollo Middle School

LIKE A BOOMERANG

Respect is like a boomerang, because if you respect someone they will respect you, like a boomerang comes right back to you. Respect is important, because if you don't respect people the respect won't come back to you like a boomerang.

Michael Williams
Two Rivers Middle School

TREAT THE SAME

Respect is to treat one group
of people the same as another.

Cole Elliott
Pearre Creek Elementary School

FROM THE HEART

Respect means to listen and obey rules, people, and the world; but true respect can't come from the mind, it has to come from the heart.

Tori Cogswell
Montgomery County Elementary School

PEACE

Respect means to me so many things:
like if everyone in the entire world had
respect for the environment, and other citizens,
the universe would be at peace. There would be no
littering, no harsh words, no one would ever get hurt.

Dani Tidwell
Westwood Elementary School

TO SUCCEED

Respect is important because without it people would not trust you to carry out tasks for them. Without respect, it is hard to succeed in life.

Nathan LaRock
Battle Ground Academy

RESPECT BRINGS LOVE

I'll hold your book while you tie your shoe!

Thanks for respecting me! I ♥ U.

Without respect we wouldn't have love, because if you don't respect anyone they won't love you or even like you.

Lundyn Coffman
Nolensville Elementary School

CONSERVE

Respect is like conserving.
If we don't conserve, all of our resources
will go away, and if we don't respect,
all of the kindness and love will go away.

Sorina Gantt
East Montgomery Elementary School

BE AMAZING

Respect means be nice to others and be an amazing person. Respect is important because if you don't have respect you won't get anywhere in life.

Anna May Clarke
Nolensville Elementary School

MANNERS MATTER!

Respect is important because it has a lot of content to it, such as: manners, trust, proper words, and more. It should be used EVERYWHERE you go and to ANYONE around you.

Ashleigh N. Stafford
Montgomery County Elementary School

HELPING OUT

Respect is helping out around your community instead of others doing it for you.

Gabriel Crucini
Scales Elementary School

RESPECT...

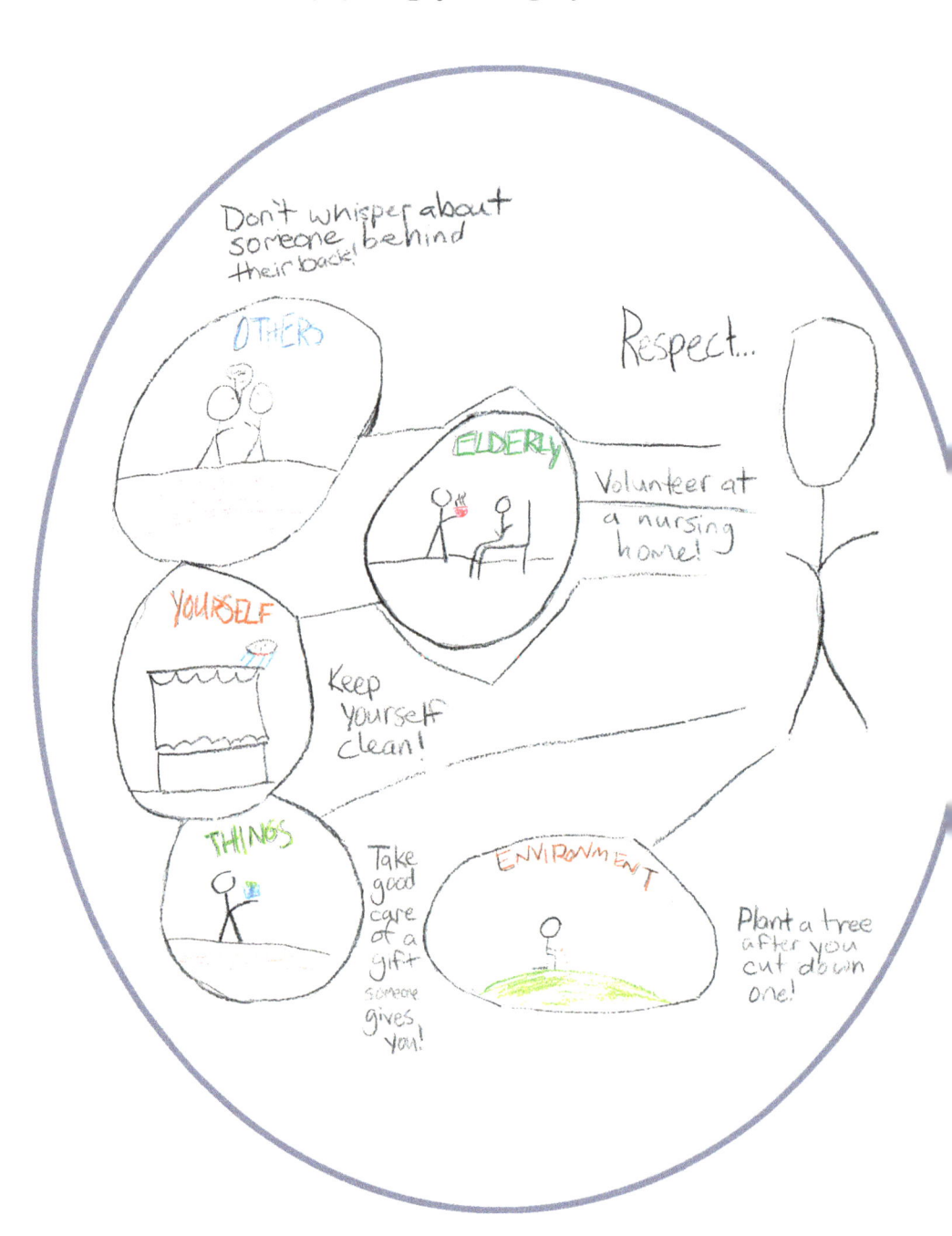

OTHERS — Don't whisper about someone behind their back!

ELDERLY — Volunteer at a nursing home!

YOURSELF — Keep yourself clean!

THINGS — Take good care of a gift someone gives you!

ENVIRONMENT — Plant a tree after you cut down one!

John Thornton
Oak Hill School

"THANK YOU!"

Welcome home U.S. army forces

"Excuse me, sir. Thank you for your service!"

"Thank you so much!"

Respect is important to everyone.
It means responsibilities, character,
integrity, and friendship.

McClain Jung
Pearre Creek Elementary School

CARING IS IMPORTANT

I think respect means caring for other people from the heart. Caring is very important when you do it from the heart.

Maggie Clark
Clarksville Academy

SHOW RESPECT, ALWAYS

Respect is a very important word.
It shows that you and/or other people know
how to act and behave to every person. Even if they
aren't nice to you, you should always have
respect toward them.

Gracie Bryant
Barksdale Elementary School

THE EARTH

I think the earth needs some respect.
So, I respect it by recycling.

Mehrab Babor
Wright Middle School

ACCEPTANCE

Respect is when you like someone for who they are.

Emeline Holt
Sunset Elementary School

APPRECIATION

I appreciate you.

And we respect you.

Troops

I think respect means to show your appreciation for someone.
Like, General Robert E. Lee and his troops:
Lee appreciated his troops, and his troops respected him back.

Lauren Block
Meigs Middle Magnet School

RESPECT THE WORLD

I think respect is being kind to others, also not littering on the ground or outside. It will help the world a lot if you do not litter, also if you are kind to others.

Ethan Hill
Westwood Elementary School

LOTS OF MEANING

Respect: A word with lots of meaning but little notice.
To me, respect is doing what you are asked (if it is right).
Without respect the world would be out of order.

Ian Reed
Nolensville Elementary School

R-E-S-P-E-C-T

What respect looks like...

"R-E-S-P-E-C-T that's what we want to Be!"

Respect means to be thoughtful and kind to whoever is speaking or doing something.

What the world would look like without respect...

Respect is important because if you don't use it the world would be a bad place to live, and you'd lose the trust of everyone.

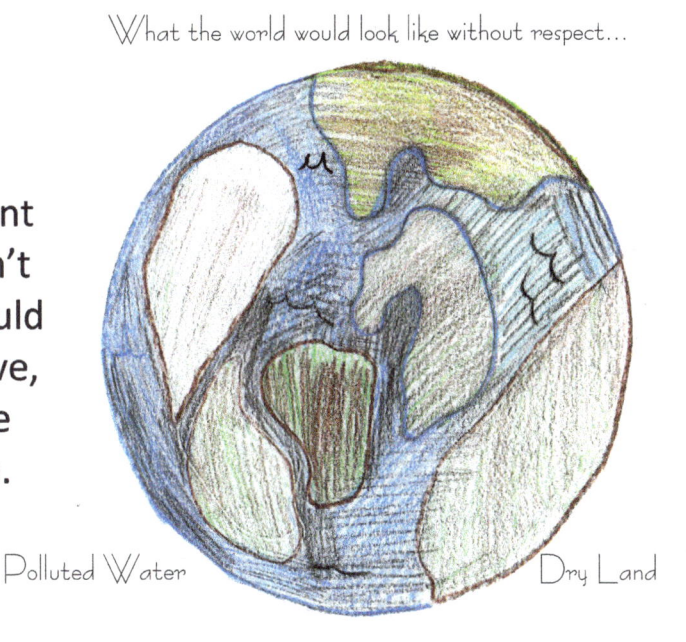

Polluted Water

Dry Land

Haley Williams
Grassland Elementary School

HONOR and CARE

Respect is important because if you don't
respect someone or something, you're basically
telling them that you don't care about them, or that
you don't care about what they're saying.
When you are respecting someone or something
you are honoring them and showing them that you care.

Annabelle Mayernick
Christ Presbyterian Academy

GIVING OTHERS SPACE

To me, respect means letting people be who they are and giving them space. Respect means treating people the way you want to be treated.

Aine M. Donohue
East Nashville Magnet School

A BETTER WORLD

Respect is a word I respect. I respect others' things, feelings, and, most importantly, them. These days respect isn't used much, with bullying going on and other stuff. Nobody should have to kill themselves because of a bully. We need to use respect more often. No more bullying, no more suicide, no more war! Everyone wants a better world than we live in now, a world with more respect.

Daniel Aglato
Bellevue Middle School

CPSIA information can be obtained
at www.ICGtesting.com
Printed in the USA
LVHW01*2149060318
568875LV00007B/9/P

9 780692 249154